The

LORD'S PRAYER

Prayer from the Heart

Jeffrey C. Smith

WHEN you are praying, do not heap up empty
   phrases as the Gentiles do; for they think that they
   will be heard because of their many words. Do
   not be like them, for your Father knows what you
   need before you ask him.

Pray then in this way:
Our Father in heaven,
   Hallowed be your name.
   Your kingdom come.
   Your will be done, on earth as it is in heaven.
   Give us this day our daily bread.
   And forgive us our debts, as we also have forgiven
   our debtors.
   And do not bring us to the time of trial,
   but rescue us from the evil one.

Matthew 6:7-13

The
LORD'S PRAYER

Prayer from the Heart

The Word Among Us

9639 Doctor Perry Road

Ijamsville, Maryland 21754

ISBN: 0-932085-15-6

© 1997 by The Word Among Us Press

Cover design by David Crosson

Made and printed in the United States of America.

Contents

Introduction

St. Matthew tells us that, even at the very beginning of his ministry, Jesus had attracted "great crowds" from all over Galilee, Jerusalem, and even the Gentile region of the Decapolis (Matthew 4:25). In this little book, we have the chance to sit with these crowds and listen to Jesus as he teaches us how to pray the Lord's Prayer (Matthew 6:9-13). Like these first disciples, we now have the freedom to call God "Father." We can approach God with the same confidence and trust that Jesus had during his life on earth.

As we practice Jesus' teaching on prayer, we can join together in worship with one another and experience a unity with the entire body of Christ. God hears us when we ask him to fill us with his love and to renew the face of the earth. Our united prayer has the power to move mountains in our world, to change nations, and to bring healing and love to all of God's creation.

Throughout church history, many of the great saints have written about the Lord's Prayer. Early Fathers of the church such as Augustine and Cyprian, and later, great theologians such as Thomas Aquinas and Teresa of Avila, have expressed not only their awe regarding this prayer, but how this simple prayer can give us a new intimacy with God and greater confidence in our relationship with him. In every age, as the faithful seek God's presence, this teaching of Jesus comes to life in their hearts.

God our Father loves hearing his children's prayers, and he invites us to pray that his kingship be established in the hearts of people in every country. He loves every person throughout the world, and it is his desire that every one of us would approach him very personally and call him "Father." As we pray this prayer together, our heavenly Father will not only fill us with love for him, but with an overflowing love for all his children throughout the world.

Jeff Smith
The Word Among Us

A Joy Rediscovered

*Through the gift of prayer,
we can be filled with the love of God.*

We've all had times when prayer feels like little more than a chore or an imposition on our busy schedule. This struggle with prayer seems to start, in fact, at an early age. Most parents have had the experience of trying to keep one or more of their children quiet during Mass as they ask, "How soon will Mass be over?" and "When can we leave?" We may find it comforting to know that we are not alone—in fact, we are in good company. Many saints throughout history experienced times when God seemed far away from them.

In this book we want to discuss how we can come to a deeper experience of the joy of prayer. We want to focus primarily on the abundant grace that flows from God's throne as his children come to worship him. It is during these times of worshipful prayer that the Holy Spirit opens us up to grace and we begin to experience the truth stated in the Catechism that "prayer comes also from the Holy Spirit" (Catechism of the Catholic Church, 2726), and doesn't arise solely from our efforts.

Perhaps the most important foundation for prayer is that we understand the one to whom we pray. There are many aspects to understanding who God is: He is without flaw or fault; he never changes his mind or makes mistakes; he is eternal and full of power; he knows everything and lacks nothing. But above all else, God's greatest attribute is his perfect love. God's love is eternal; it existed long before we were born; it will never wane. It is a love that brings freedom and joy to his children. It is a love which moved him to reveal himself to humanity, to invite each individual person into a relationship of love with him. "Knowing" God must include experiencing this immense love as it flows from the heart of the Trinity.

At its most basic—and its most profound—level, prayer is coming into contact with God, who is love. God's heartfelt love can be seen most clearly in the Father's relationship with Jesus, the Son. In the New Testament letter to the Colossians, we read that in Christ "all the fullness of God was pleased to dwell" (Colossians 1:19). The Father loves the Son so fully that he eternally pours into him his entire being, the fullness of his life.

Out of his love for the Son, the Father brought forth the whole of creation, including man and woman. In Christ, and from all eternity, the Father knows and loves every one of us. When he called Jeremiah, the Lord said, "Before I formed you in the womb I knew you, and before you were born I consecrated you" (Jeremiah 1:5). The psalmist also prayed: "You formed my inward parts, you knit me together in my mother's womb. . . . My frame was not hidden from you, when I was being made in secret. . . . In your book were written, every one of them, the days that were formed for me, when as yet there was none of them. How precious to me are your thoughts, O God! How vast is the sum of them!" (Psalm 139:13,15-17).

Throughout History

Throughout his public ministry, Jesus reflected this perfect love of the Father and his desire to gather his people to himself. At the last supper, Jesus told his disciples: "I have earnestly desired to eat this passover with you before I suffer" (Luke 22:15). The Greek word for desire here, *epithumia*, speaks of a passionate longing, a heart that is fully set upon a goal. This is the kind of love which burns in Jesus for his people.

In the history of the church, God continues to reveal himself as a Father whose desire is to call his children together and form them into his own special possession. We can see this in the life of St. Augustine, who experienced God's love pursuing him even when he was engaged in a sinful relationship or entangled in heresy. Despite these obstacles, the Father continued to pursue Augustine, to draw him to himself. And God finally won, as Augustine recognized later in his life:

> Late have I loved you, beauty so old and so new:
> Late have I loved you. . . . You were with me, and
> I was not with you. . . . You called and cried out
> loud and shattered my deafness. You were radiant
> and resplendent, you put to flight my blindness.
> You were fragrant, and I drew in my breath and
> now pant after you. I tasted you, and I feel but
> hunger and thirst for you. You touched me, and I
> am set on fire to attain the peace which is yours.
> (*Confessions*, 10.27)

In his desire to draw all his children to himself, God looks for hearts which will say "yes" to him. St. Francis of Assisi is a marvelous demonstration of how a simple "yes" can affect the whole church. When Francis first heard God's call to build his church, he couldn't see how to respond except by trying to repair the ramshackle little church of San Damiano. But Francis' obedient "yes" allowed God to bring forth a great renewal of the church in the thirteenth century. Today, God is still active and dynamic in his desire to draw us to himself, and it is through prayer that we are touched by this longing of God.

Sitting at Jesus' Feet

Quoting from the Gospel of John, the Catholic Catechism speaks of the grace that flows from heaven when we come to pray:

"If you knew the gift of God!" The wonder of prayer is revealed beside the well where we come seeking water: there, Christ comes to meet every human being. It is he who first seeks us and asks us for a drink. Jesus thirsts; his asking arises from the depths of God's desire for us. Whether we realize it or not, prayer is the encounter of God's thirst with ours. God thirsts that we may thirst for him. (CCC, 2560; John 4:10)

God wants us to look on prayer not as a burden, but

as a response of love. We love God and long to be with him because he first loved us (1 John 4:9-10). Prayer is meant to have this two-fold aspect: We receive the love of the Father, and we draw closer to him and love him in return.

The story of Martha and Mary illustrates the attitude that is so pleasing to Jesus (Luke 10:38-42). While both sisters were eager to welcome Jesus into their home, Mary put aside her temporal concerns to sit at his feet and listen to his teaching. Jesus was pleased with her attitude and commended her for it, telling Martha that Mary had chosen the better path. Of course, Jesus doesn't want us to neglect our responsibilities, but he delights in teaching his children when they set aside time to sit at his feet and listen to his voice.

Another gospel story in which we see someone at Jesus' feet is the story of the sinful woman who anointed Jesus (Luke 7:36-50). This woman was not constrained by others' opinions of her, even though she knew she would face opposition from the Pharisees. Her desire for Jesus overwhelmed any fear of ridicule. How happy Jesus must have been when she washed his feet with her tears and dried them with her hair—before she anointed him with costly perfume.

The last time we see people at Jesus' feet is at Calvary, when his mother and John, the beloved disciple, gazed on him as he hung on the cross (John 19:26). They saw his blood flowing from him, bringing forgiveness and healing to all humanity. They witnessed Jesus fulfilling his own words: "Greater love has no man than this, that a man lay down his life for his friends" (John 15:13).

Like each of these believers, we too are invited to sit at Jesus' feet as we come to him in prayer each day. As we sit before him and ponder his word to us, Jesus will teach us just as he taught Martha's sister Mary. When we worship Jesus in our personal prayer, we express our love and gratitude. We pour out our lives to him, much as the sinful woman offered her treasure to Jesus. And as Jesus' mother and his beloved disciple witnessed his sacrifice of love, we too can receive his body and blood in the

Eucharist and celebrate his love for us, his friends.

Power to Transform and Renew

When God's children come into his presence, lives begin to change. The person who relies solely on scientific proof may see prayer as having a "placebo effect," that is, it benefits only those who want to believe that prayer works. With eyes of faith, however, Christians see what cannot be proven scientifically—that the heavenly Father hears every prayer and pours out his grace on those who seek him with all their heart (Jeremiah 29:13).

It is in prayer that struggles and problems the size of mountains can be moved. The story of Job demonstrates how a person who comes into God's presence can be dramatically transformed. Job's troubles were overwhelming: He lost everything he owned; his children all died tragically; he was tormented by disease. After a long struggle with friends who tried in vain to counsel him, Job experienced the presence of God (Job 38-42). All his anxieties about his state, all his bitterness against God, all his lamenting, came to an end as he responded: "I had heard of you by the hearing of the ear, but now my eye sees you" (Job 42:5).

Our lives can be transformed as we experience God's love and presence in prayer. Fears, confusion, hatred, and bondage to sin will yield to the power and love of God. In prayer, we are intimately united with Christ; therefore, we begin to love as he loved, to forgive as he forgave, to turn away from temptation as he did, and to rely on the Father as he did. Prayer transforms our being so that we can claim with Paul: "It is no longer I who live, but Christ who lives in me" (Galatians 2:20).

Our Hidden Center
Words from the Catechism

THE HEART IS THE DWELLING-PLACE where I am, where I live; according to the Semitic or biblical expression, the heart is the place "to which I withdraw." The heart is our hidden center, beyond the grasp of our reason and of others; only the Spirit of God can fathom the human heart and know it fully. The heart is the place of decision, deeper than our psychic drives. It is the place of truth where we choose life or death. It is the place of encounter, because as image of God we live in relation; it is the place of covenant. (CCC, 2563)

In the New Covenant, prayer is the living relationship of the children of God with their Father who is good beyond measure, with his Son Jesus Christ and with the Holy Spirit. The grace of the Kingdom is "the union of the entire holy and royal Trinity . . . with the whole human spirit." Thus, the life of prayer is the habit of being in the presence of the thrice-holy God and in communion with him. This communion of life is always possible because through Baptism, we have already been united with Christ. Prayer is *Christian* insofar as it is communion with Christ and extends throughout the Church, which is his Body. Its dimensions are those of Christ's love. (CCC, 2565)

Our Father

*It is our great privilege as Christians
to call God "Father."*

Imagine yourself as one of Jesus' followers, sitting in a field in Galilee, surrounded by hundreds, maybe even thousands of others, listening attentively to him speaking. Along with everyone else, you are captivated by his wisdom and authority; you have the feeling that there is something special about this man. Even apart from the reports of miracles and healings, you are moved as you hear him speak about God as a Father. This rabbi is not like the others. He speaks about God from a personal perspective. His heart seems so filled with God's love that it just pours out of him into others, for them to accept or reject.

You are especially struck by his words on prayer, as he

tells his listeners that they can call God their Father, just as he does. You sense that in this prayer, Jesus is not only giving you words to memorize and recite; he is revealing his heart to you and inviting you to share in his love for the Father. He would not be teaching you to say these words if he did not know that this kind of relationship with God is possible. With great hope and expectation, you listen closely to his words.

"Abba! Father!"

St. Paul taught that at baptism God gives us his Spirit, who constantly calls out "Abba! Father!" in our hearts (Galatians 4:6). What a privilege we have received: The omnipotent and holy God has adopted us as his own children and invites us to call him, "Father." Some of us may have a father who was a good role model of God the Father—offering us a healthy balance between compassion and discipline, between guidance and personal responsibility. Such a father would have provided a sense of security and stability to our lives; he would have been instrumental in forming our consciences and teaching us the gospel in a living way.

Others, however, may not have had such a fine example. In fact, some may have experienced pain or abuse as a result of their relationship with their fathers. In a special way, the Lord's Prayer offers these people an opportunity to come to know a Father who will never let them down, one who is there for them whenever they call out, one who longs to shelter them in his arms and protect them. Learning to call God "Father" can bring great healing to wounds from our past and equip us to face the future with the security and peace that come from knowing a father's love.

For all of us, the Our Father gives us an opportunity to know in a new way the innocence and freedom of children: "A humble and trusting heart . . . enables us to turn and become like children; for it is to little children that the Father is revealed" (CCC, 2785). Think of the trust and abandonment which a little child has at home, the confidence in approaching his or her father knowing that he or she will be listened to and loved. Think, too, of the reliance that children have on their parents, their willingness to believe them, simply because they have experienced—in very tangible ways—their parents' love and provision.

Finally, by calling God Our Father, we learn the value and importance of a family identity. Not only are we children of God, we are also brothers and sisters to one another, "members of the household of God" (Ephesians 2:19):

> If we pray the Our Father sincerely, we leave individualism behind, because the love that we receive frees us from it. The "our" at the beginning of the Lord's Prayer, like the "us" of the last four petitions, excludes no one. If we are to say it truthfully, our divisions and oppositions have to be overcome. (CCC, 2792)

All of these analogies give us wonderful insights and sincere hope in everything God wants us to experience

in our life with him. God does not want us to think of
him as far off from us; he wants us to know his love and
to feel free to come to him in prayer. He wants us to have
confidence in his provision for our lives, to experience
the transformation and grace that are available to us as
the children he has redeemed through his beloved Son,
Jesus.

Holy Is Your Name . . .

God delights in revealing his holiness to us as we
come to him in prayer. His goal is not to impress us, or to
intimidate us into obedience. Rather, by giving us a
glimpse of his majesty and mercy and glory, he wants to
enkindle in our hearts a greater love for him and a deeper
gratitude for the life he has given us in Christ. In the book
of Revelation, all the members of the heavenly court are
privileged to see the Lord in all his glory and power.
Moved by the vision, they all bow down in worship, cry-
ing out: "Worthy are you, our Lord and God, to receive

glory and honor and power, for you created all things, and by your will they existed and were created" (Revelation 4:11). Then, upon seeing Jesus, the Lamb of God who still bears the marks of his wounds—only now glorified—they sing: "Worthy is the Lamb who was slain, to receive power and wealth and wisdom and might and honor and glory and blessing!" (5:12).

When we perceive even the smallest glimpse of God's glory—whether through the beauty of creation, the intimacy of loving family relationships, or through contemplating Christ on the cross—our hearts are moved naturally to respond with worship and adoration. Like the elders in Revelation, something moves us to "cast our crowns" before God, offering him our lives and opening our hearts to embrace his will (Revelation 4:10).

This movement toward God is the heart of worship; it is expressed in our prayer that God's name—his very Person—be revered and praised for his holiness and perfection. Such worship comes as we begin to recognize God's hand in all of creation, and especially in our own lives. It wells up within us, and—although it may be a very small, quiet voice—the more we yield to it, the greater it becomes, and the more our hearts are filled with his love and a desire to receive even more from him.

Your Kingdom Come . . .

At the incarnation, the Son of God entered into time and space to proclaim that the kingdom of God was near at hand (Mark 1:15). A significant part of Jesus' earthly ministry was to allow men and women to experience the reality of this kingdom: Good news proclaimed to the poor and outcast; repentance and reconciliation for those bound in sin; healing for the sick; miracles displayed to the unbelieving (Matthew 11:4; Luke 4:18-19). With all these signs, is it any wonder that when Jesus entered Jerusalem on Palm Sunday, the crowds called out: "Blessed is the kingdom of our father David that is coming!" (Mark 11:10)?

Jesus himself prayed, "Thy kingdom come." He knew

he had come to establish the kingdom of God; his death and resurrection would bring the first fruits of this kingdom. Yet he also knew that his Father's kingdom would not come in fullness until the day when he would return in glory, bringing to completion his triumph over sin and death. More than anyone else, Jesus longed for the fullness of God's reign, for the time when the church would finally be brought to the Father in all its splendor and power, and filled with the glory of the Spirit.

It is a sure sign that the Spirit is working in us when we find ourselves looking forward to the day when we will see Jesus face to face (1 John 3:2-3). Commenting on this part of the Lord's Prayer, the early Christian theologian Tertullian wrote: "Even if it had not been prescribed to pray for the coming of the kingdom, we would willingly have brought forth this speech, eager to embrace our hope" (On Prayer, 5). What beauty, what joy, what love will be ours at this time! It is no wonder that scripture ends with the eager shout, "Come, Lord Jesus!" (Revelation 22:20).

Your Will Be Done. . .

More than any other person, Mary could have taught Jesus to pray "Thy will be done." This prayer, which was in her heart from her earliest days, found its greatest expression as she accepted the angel's words about the child to be born to her: "Behold, I am the handmaid of the Lord; let it be to me according to your word" (Luke 1:38). Like his mother, Jesus learned to pray this way, not reluctantly, but trusting that his Father's will was more to be desired than his own human will. In Gethsemane, at the most trying time of his life, Jesus was able to pray this prayer. He had prayed it so frequently throughout his life that it had become a part of him. Even in the deepest anguish of his soul he could say: "Father, if you are willing, remove this cup from me; nevertheless not my will, but yours, be done" (Luke 22:42).

We may find it comforting to know that this prayer is not something we are able to pray through our own power. Rather, the Spirit of God—whom we received at baptism—is the one who enables us to speak these words from the heart: "We are radically incapable of this, but united with Jesus and with the power of his Holy Spirit, we can surrender our will to him and decide to choose what his Son has always chosen: to do what is pleasing to the Father" (CCC, 2825).

If we find ourselves resistant to this prayer, we must not allow ourselves to be discouraged. Instead, we should ask God to enable us to fall in love with his will for our lives— just as Jesus, Mary, and all the saints learned to do. As we practice this prayer in the little decisions we face each day, we will find our hearts more able to pray this way during times of trial and difficulty.

The Innocence of Children

In the Our Father, Jesus has given us a way of prayer that opens us up to a loving relationship with God, our heavenly Father. This prayer can bring us great healing and comfort as we experience the innocence and freedom of children whose lives are in their Father's loving hands.

Roots of the Lord's Prayer

THIS PRAYER THAT JESUS taught us is rooted in the Jewish liturgical traditions of his day, especially the Qaddish, a prayer that was recited regularly at synagogues in the first century A.D.:

> *Exalted and hallowed be His great Name*
> > *In the world which He created*
> > *According to His will.*
> *May He establish His kingdom*
> > *In your lifetime and in your days,*
> > *And in the lifetime of the whole household of Israel,*
> > *Speedily and at a near time.*
> *Amen.*

Raised in the ways of God's chosen people, Jesus took their traditions and filled them with the light of divine revelation. Thus, not only were the Jewish traditions preserved; they were transformed and elevated to reflect the new covenant that God offers all people through his Son.

Give Us This
Day Our Daily Bread

*God delights in caring for his children.
How can we begin to trust in him?*

Jesus taught his disciples to receive from God every day, without cost. Our Father, who loves us so, delights to give us—freely—everything we need to stay close to him, to obey him, and to serve him and his people each day. During the Israelites' forty years in the desert, God fed them every day with manna from heaven. They were told to gather only enough for the day; whatever they had left over would spoil the next morning (Exodus 16:19-21). In this way, God taught his children how reliable he is—that he would never fail them, no matter what challenge they might face.

God wants us to learn this same kind of daily reliance on him for his strength, his love, and his wisdom to guide our lives. It is not uncommon today to hear that we need to be self-reliant, to trust no one with our lives, to be quick to end relationships that get too demanding. While it is good to have a healthy sense of self-confidence, this self-reliance we often hear touted can lead us to avoid trusting in the Father and his perfect plan for our lives.

Our "daily bread" comes to us in many ways. The Eucharist itself is one of the greatest gifts the Lord gives us. Like the Israelites in the desert, we do not earn Jesus' presence; he loves us so much that he offers it freely to us. As we receive Jesus' body and blood, his very life flows into our hearts, transforming us into his likeness and drawing us together as his people, his body on earth. This gift has many dimensions. It can bring healing and peace to every aspect of our lives if we approach the Lord in faith, seeking the nourishment that he deeply desires to give us.

Following the tradition of the Israelites, Jesus linked the image of bread with the word of God: "It is written, 'Man shall not live by bread alone, but by every word that proceeds from the mouth of God' " (Matthew 4:4; see Deuteronomy 8:3). Amos, the shepherd-turned-prophet, also prophesied: "I will send a famine on the land; not a famine of bread, nor a thirst for water, but of hearing the words of the LORD" (Amos 8:11). God wants to speak his word into our hearts every day, feeding us with his wisdom and refreshing us with his presence. What would you do if one of your children were in a land of terrible famine right now, suffering from thirst and hunger? Wouldn't your love compel you to go to him or her with food and drink? In a similar way, our Father laments over his children who are not filled with his words of life and comfort.

Forgive Us . . . As We Forgive . . .

This can be the most difficult part of the Our Father for us to pray. Like any good father, God wants all his children to love one another. Just as Jesus freely poured out his blood at Calvary to forgive all our sins, he calls us to forgive, just as freely, all those who have sinned against us. Jesus doesn't tell us that we need to wait for people to come and ask our forgiveness. Just as our Father forgave us before we were even born, we are to forgive others and not hold them bound.

This truth applies especially to family life. We are capable of causing the most pain to those we are closest to, simply because we share so much of our lives with each other. As we learn to practice love and forgiveness in our homes, however, our own hearts will be softened; we will be opened up more fully to the great mercy that God has for us. It is the power of God which enables us to forgive—which releases us from the bitterness, fear, or anger that are often the result of having been sinned against. One who is filled with Christ's love and presence is able to pray: "Lord, I forgive this person. I don't hold them bound by what they did to me. Let your mercy cover and protect us both." The Catechism teaches that it is "in the depths of the heart that everything is bound and loosed. It is not in our power not to feel or to forget an offense; but the heart that offers itself to the Holy Spirit turns injury into compassion and purifies the memory in transforming the hurt into intercession" (CCC, 2843).

Jesus lived out this prayer of forgiveness most fully when he prayed from the cross: "Father, forgive them; for they know not what they do" (Luke 23:34). This prayer encompassed his close friends—those who denied and betrayed him—as well as his enemies—those who conspired to subject him to such a death. In his immense love as shown by his prayer for his enemies, Jesus gave us a living example of the richness of God's mercy and the depth of transformation that can occur in us as our prayer deepens. As the Catechism teaches:

> Christian prayer extends to the forgiveness of enemies, transfiguring the disciple by configuring him to his Master. Forgiveness is a highpoint of Christian prayer; only hearts attuned to God's compassion can receive the gift of

prayer. Forgiveness also bears witness that, in our world, love is stronger than sin. (CCC, 2844)

Lead Us Not Into Temptation . . .

During his lifetime, Jesus experienced the fiercest temptations anyone could know. Immediately after his baptism by John, he was led by the Spirit into the desert, where the evil one enticed him to fail in his love and obedience to his Father. The devil tried to sway him by offering him creature comforts, a position of worldly honor and glory; material wealth; and a demonstration of power (Matthew 4:1-11). The devil chose a time when Jesus was physically weak and when his mental and emotional defenses would have been most vulnerable, thinking that he could win on these grounds. Yet in his heart—in the secret place where the Spirit of holiness dwells—Jesus continued to rely on his Father. He did not succumb to Satan's wiles.

From this experience of relying on his Father and thereby defeating the devil, Jesus taught his disciples the secret of victory over temptation. Like our Master, we too must rely on the Father in our hearts so that we can withstand temptation and avoid the seductions of the evil one. The same Spirit who strengthened Jesus dwells in us, his sanctuary is in our hearts as well. There, he offers us the love and presence of the Father; through faith and reliance on the Father's love, we too have the power to conquer the evil one. As St. Paul encouraged the Roman Christians, he teaches us as well: "In all these things we are more than conquerors through him who loved us" (Romans 8:37). In the book of Revelation, Jesus himself promised a great inheritance to those who overcome (Revelation 2:7,11,17,26; 3:5,12,21). In dealing with temptation, we must learn a whole new way of overcoming, the way of prayer:

It is by his prayer that Jesus vanquishes the tempter, both at the outset of his public mission and in the ultimate struggle of his agony. In this petition to our heavenly Father, Christ unites us to his battle and his agony. He urges us to *vigilance* of the heart in communion with his own. Vigilance is "custody of the heart," and Jesus prayed for us to the Father: "Keep them in your name." The Holy Spirit constantly seeks to awaken us to keep watch. (CCC, 2849)

As we learn to wait on the Lord and remain in his presence, we will be given the ability to recognize temptations when they come our way. We will become increasingly confident in our Father's ability to protect us and keep us safe (see CCC, 2847).

But Deliver Us From Evil

Today, in a world blessed with great scientific discoveries and technological advancements, some men and women have adopted a skeptical philosophy that says, "I must see it to believe it." Such thinking can turn us away from a position of faith. It can lead us to doubt the existence of that spiritual "realm" which both transcends our senses and yet can have a great effect on the way we live. In fact, one of the greatest deceptions of the devil in this age is to blind us to the reality of the spiritual battle in which we are engaged—to tempt us to deny his existence at all:

> Evil is not an abstraction, but refers to a person, Satan, the Evil One, the angel who opposes God. The devil is the one who "throws himself across" God's plan and his work of salvation accomplished in Christ. (CCC, 2851)

Scripture, too, is clear about the reality of the evil one: "We are not contending against flesh and blood, but against the principalities, against the powers, against the world rulers of this present darkness, against the spiritual hosts of wickedness in the heavenly places" (Ephesians 6:12). Those who recognize the reality of this spiritual warfare find themselves drawn to Jesus' feet. There they are protected and guided so that the evil one cannot harm them. It is at Jesus' feet that we receive "the whole armor of God" (6:13) and learn how effective it is in combatting the enemy. We can be confident when we come to Christ for protection and strength, because his victory is already complete, and we have been baptized into this victory.

Kingdom, Power, and Glory

Throughout his ministry, Jesus spoke constantly about his Father, revealing God's love and compassion for everyone. This is especially true in the Sermon on the Mount, which gave believers a new way to look at God—not as a vindictive and arbitrary judge, but as a loving Father who knows every hair on our heads, who feeds and clothes those who seek his kingdom above all else, who delights in giving good things to those who ask him.

In the Our Father, Jesus has shown us what it is like to have an intimate relationship with his Father. Through his death and resurrection, he has invited us into this relationship as the result of our union with him. When he rose on Easter Sunday, Jesus gave Mary Magdalene a message for Peter and the other apostles: "Say to them, I am ascending to my Father and your Father, to my God and your God" (John 20:17). Because of Jesus' resurrection from the dead, we now have the privilege of calling God "Father." The uncreated Creator, to whom belongs the kingdom, the power, and the glory of all the universe, is our Father, and he delights in calling us his beloved sons and daughters.

Bread from the Lord
Words from St. Augustine

WE SHOULD UNDERSTAND the daily bread as
spiritual, that is to say, divine precepts, which we
ought to meditate on and to labor after every day.
For just with respect to these the Lord says,
"Labor for the food that does not perish." That
food is called daily food at present, so long as
this temporal life is measured off by days that
depart and return. And, in truth, as long as the
desire of the soul is directed by turns, now to
what is higher, now to what is lower, i.e., now to
spiritual things, now to carnal, . . . bread is daily
necessary, in order that the hungry man may be
recruited, and he who is falling down may be
raised up.

(On the Lord's Sermon on the Mount, 7.27)

A
GUIDE
TO
PRAYER

CHOOSE A TIME.

Make it a definite time dedicated only to prayer. Try to make it the best time for prayer you can find.

CHOOSE A PLACE.

It should be free from distractions.

ENTER INTO PRAYER.

Examine your conscience and repent of your sins.
(*Matthew 5:23-24; 6:14-15; Psalm 51:1-5; Psalm 130*)

Let God's mercy cleanse your conscience.
(*Romans 8:32; Hebrews 9:14*)

Lay aside anxieties, problems, struggles.

Do not allow your troubles to dominate your time with God; he is Lord of all. (*Hebrews 12:1-2*)

OPEN YOUR HEART TO THE TRUTHS OF THE GOSPEL.

God created you out of love and loves you always.
(*Genesis 1:27-31; 1 John 4:10-11*)

God sent Jesus to give us life. (*John 3:16; Ephesians 2:4-5*)

Jesus died and rose, conquering sin and death.
(*Romans 5:12-18; 1 Corinthians 15:22-26*)

Jesus promised to be with us and to send the Holy Spirit. *(John 14:16; 14:26; 16:7; Acts 2:1-4)*

Jesus intercedes for us in heaven. *(Romans 8:34; Hebrews 7:25; 1 John 2:1)*

Jesus is coming again. *(Matthew 16:27; 25:34)*

Consciously say "Yes" to these truths each day.

PRAISE GOD.

He is worthy of all praise. *(Psalm 95; 136; 150; Hebrews 13:15; 1 Peter 2:9)*

Express your love and gratitude to our Father, to his Son Jesus, and to the Holy Spirit of Truth.

Speak with God honestly and from the heart.

ASK QUESTIONS. *(Matthew 7:7-11)*

Listen actively to God in your heart and mind as you read scripture or kneel before him.

Reflect on his word.

Dwell in the presence of God.

INTERCEDE WITH FAITH AND TRUST.

For daily bread: Pray for the world, the church, your friends, family, yourself.

For forgiveness: As you forgive others.

For strength for the day and its trials.

For protection from all evil.

BEFORE LEAVING PRAYER WRITE DOWN:

What God has said to you.

What he has shown you.

What you want to carry into the day and remember so that your prayer will bear fruit.

What you have prayed for.